KAREN LATCHANA KENNEY

THE SCIENCE OF GLACIERS

HOW TEMPERATURE WORKS

Checkerboard
Library

An Imprint of Abdo Publishing
abdopublishing.com

abdopublishing.com

Published by Abdo Publishing, a division of ABDO, PO Box 398166, Minneapolis, Minnesota 55439. Copyright © 2016 by Abdo Consulting Group, Inc. International copyrights reserved in all countries. No part of this book may be reproduced in any form without written permission from the publisher. Checkerboard Library™ is a trademark and logo of Abdo Publishing.

Printed in the United States of America, North Mankato, Minnesota

102015
012016

THIS BOOK CONTAINS
RECYCLED MATERIALS

Design: Christa Schneider
Production: Mighty Media. Inc.
Editor: Liz Salzmann

Cover Photos: Shutterstock, front cover, back cover
Interior Photos: iStockphoto, pp. 20, 27; Mighty Media, Inc., pp. 4–5, 7, 9, 13, 19, 23; NASA/SDO, p. 12; Shutterstock, pp. 6, 8, 10, 13, 14, 15, 17, 18, 21, 23, 25, 26, 28–29; The Natural History Museum/Alamy, p. 11

Library of Congress Cataloging-in-Publication Data

Kenney, Karen Latchana, author.
  The science of glaciers : how temperature works / Karen Latchana Kenney.
    pages cm. -- (Science in action)
  Includes index.
  ISBN 978-1-62403-961-4
1. Glaciers--Juvenile literature. 2. Glaciology--Juvenile literature. I. Title.
  GB2403.8.K46 2016
  551.31ʼ2--dc23
                    2015026212

CONTENTS

WATCH OUT!
ICEBERG!

Loud groans and moans echo through the water. Something is happening deep inside the glacier. Suddenly a massive piece of ice breaks off. It falls into the sea with a huge splash. It drifts away from its frozen home. This floating ice is a new iceberg.

4

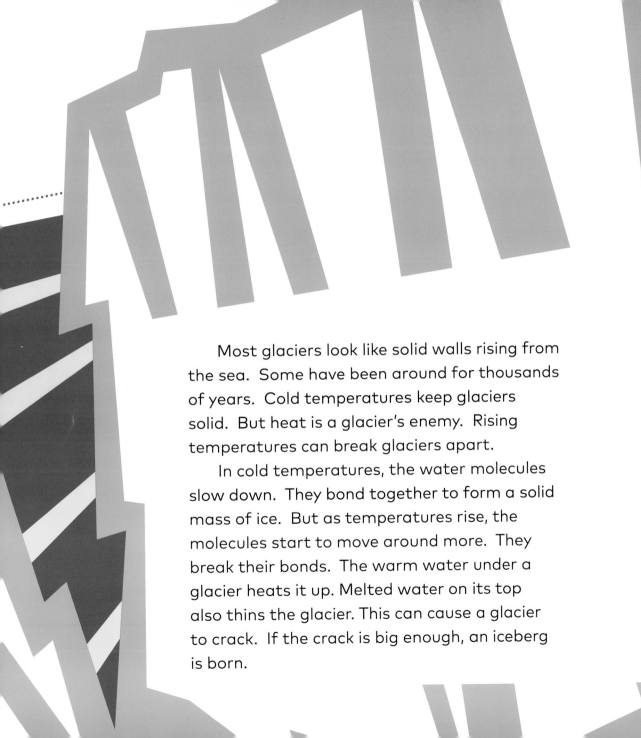

Most glaciers look like solid walls rising from the sea. Some have been around for thousands of years. Cold temperatures keep glaciers solid. But heat is a glacier's enemy. Rising temperatures can break glaciers apart.

In cold temperatures, the water molecules slow down. They bond together to form a solid mass of ice. But as temperatures rise, the molecules start to move around more. They break their bonds. The warm water under a glacier heats it up. Melted water on its top also thins the glacier. This can cause a glacier to crack. If the crack is big enough, an iceberg is born.

WHAT IS TEMPERATURE?

CHAPTER 1

Step outside and feel the heat of the sun's rays. It's what makes Earth's temperatures rise and fall. Heat is a form of energy. It can come from light, like the sun's heat. It can also come from other sources. Electricity and **friction** cause heat. So does **combustion**.

The sun is a natural source of heat.

Temperature is the measurement of the amount of heat energy in an object. When heat transfers from one object to another, the temperature of each object changes. Usually heat moves from a hotter object to a colder object. This makes the hotter object have a lower temperature. The colder object's temperature goes up.

THERMOMETERS AND TEMPERATURE SCALES

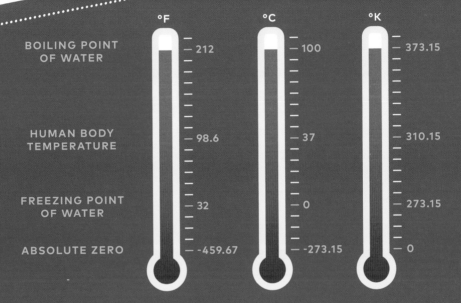

	°F	°C	°K
BOILING POINT OF WATER	212	100	373.15
HUMAN BODY TEMPERATURE	98.6	37	310.15
FREEZING POINT OF WATER	32	0	273.15
ABSOLUTE ZERO	-459.67	-273.15	0

A thermometer measures temperature. It uses a temperature scale. There are three main scales. The Fahrenheit scale (°F) is used most often in the United States. The Celsius scale (°C) is used in countries that use the metric system. The Kelvin scale (°K) is used in science.

Each scale shows a different measurement for the same temperature. Imagine a pot of water on the stove. It gets hotter and hotter until it starts boiling. This boiling point is 212 degrees Fahrenheit, 100 degrees Celsius, and 373.15 degrees Kelvin. The temperature of the water is the same. It's the number assigned to it that varies.

TINY
ATOMS

Everything in the universe is made of atoms. An atom is the smallest unit of matter. All atoms have the same basic structure. At an atom's center is the nucleus. It contains protons and neutrons. Protons have a positive electrical charge. Neutrons have no electrical charge.

The way light reflects off dense ice makes some glaciers look blue.

Electrons surround the nucleus. They have a negative electrical charge.

Each atom contains the properties of a chemical element, such as **hydrogen** or oxygen. Atoms bond with each other to form molecules. A water molecule is two hydrogen atoms and one oxygen atom bonded together. A glacier is made mostly of frozen water molecules.

ATOMIC STRUCTURE

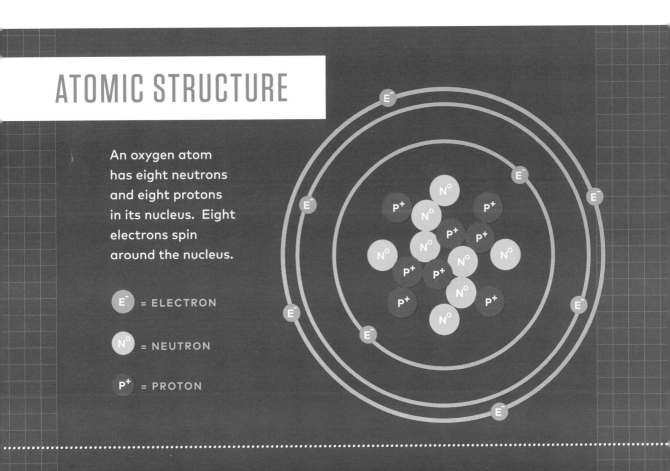

An oxygen atom has eight neutrons and eight protons in its nucleus. Eight electrons spin around the nucleus.

E⁻ = ELECTRON

N⁰ = NEUTRON

P⁺ = PROTON

MOVING MOLECULES

Molecules are always moving. They speed up or slow down depending on the energy around them. A glacier absorbs heat energy from the sun and warm ocean water. This causes its water molecules to move faster and faster. Their combined energy heats up the glacier.

The faster the molecules move, the hotter the glacier gets. The glacier begins to melt. Removing the heat energy surrounding the glacier slows down its molecules. The glacier freezes solid again.

The sun shines on a glacier in Paradise Bay, Antarctica.

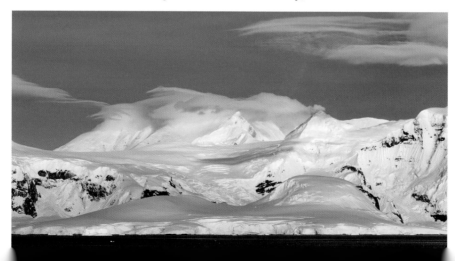

ROBERT BROWN

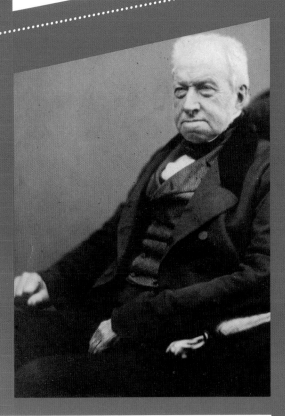

Scottish scientist Robert Brown was born in 1773. He studied small particles in liquid. Brown noticed that the particles **randomly** moved. Higher temperatures increased the motion. He published his observations in 1828. The particle motion he described became known as "Brownian motion." Later scientists, including Albert Einstein, improved on Brown's theory. A powerful microscope was invented in 1903. It allowed scientists to see the particles in more detail. In the 1920s, French scientist Jean-Baptiste Perrin proved that atoms and molecules exist.

Robert Brown was one of the first scientists to use a microscope to study plants.

ENERGY SOURCE

Earth gets energy from the sun. The sun's energy controls Earth's climate. The land, ocean, and atmosphere all absorb the sun's light energy. This energy keeps bodies of water liquid. It allows plants to grow. It melts snow and ice. And it warms Earth's temperatures.

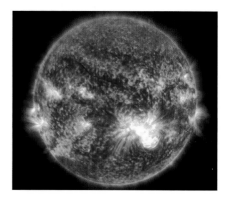

Sudden releases of extra energy cause bright spots on the sun. They are called solar flares.

Since Earth is a **sphere**, the sun's light does not hit all parts of Earth equally. The sun's light hits the area near the equator most directly. The heat energy is concentrated in a small area. So it gets hottest there.

The Earth's surface curves above and below the equator. This causes the sun's light to hit those areas at an angle. The heat energy is spread over a larger area. So it doesn't get as hot.

The angle of the Earth's surface is greatest at the North Pole and South Pole. The heat energy is spread out the most there. So they are the coldest parts of Earth. Because of this, most glaciers are in the Arctic and Antarctic.

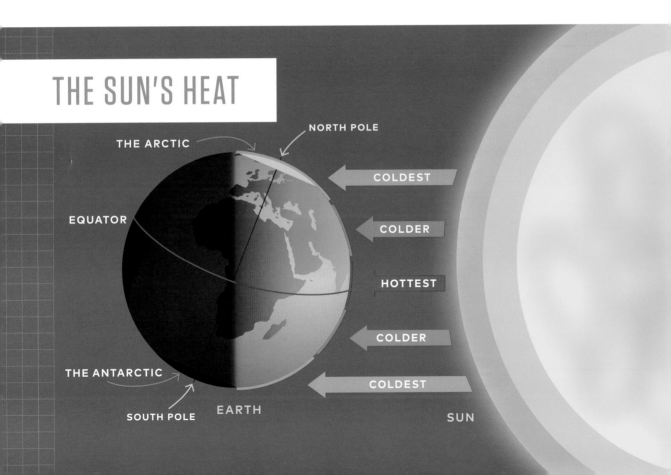

THE SUN'S HEAT

NORTH POLE

THE ARCTIC

COLDEST

COLDER

EQUATOR

HOTTEST

COLDER

THE ANTARCTIC

COLDEST

SOUTH POLE   EARTH

SUN

CHANGING STATES

There are three main states of matter. It can be a solid, a liquid, or a gas. Molecules act differently in each state.

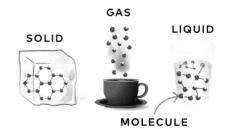

Three states of water

Solids have a specific shape and a fixed volume. So in a solid, molecules are packed closely together. A glacier is water in its solid form.

As a glacier warms, some of it becomes liquid. Liquid takes on the shape of its container. It also keeps its volume. So in liquids, molecules have space to **bounce** around more, but are still close together.

If a glacier gets hot enough, some of its water turns into gas. Gaseous water is called water vapor or steam. A gas has no size or shape. Free of these restrictions, its molecules rapidly bounce around in no specific order.

SCIENTIST AND INVENTOR
DANIEL FAHRENHEIT

Daniel Fahrenheit was born in Poland in 1686. He later moved to the Netherlands and became a **physicist**. In the early 1700s, Fahrenheit invented the alcohol and **mercury** thermometers. He also created the Fahrenheit temperature scale. Fahrenheit made many important discoveries about temperature and states of matter. One was that sometimes water remains liquid below its freezing point. Fahrenheit died in 1736.

A mercury thermometer using the Fahrenheit scale

GETTING
COLD

If the temperature around an object is colder than the object's heat transfers out. The object becomes colder. If a liquid gets cold enough, it reaches its freezing point and turns into a solid.

Water's freezing point is 32 degrees Fahrenheit (0°C). In order for water to stay solid, the temperature around it must stay at or below that temperature. That's why glaciers form where it is always very cold.

Antarctica is the coldest part of Earth. Its average temperature is –18 degrees Fahrenheit (–28.2°C) in summer and –76 degrees Fahrenheit (–60°C) in winter. But on the East Antarctic Plateau, the temperature can fall below –133.6 degrees Fahrenheit (–92°C) in winter.

Antarctica has more ice than anywhere else. Nearly 85 percent of Earth's ice is found in Antarctica's glaciers. The ice there can be 15,420 feet (4,700 m) thick!

Land under Antarctic glaciers helps keep the ice extremely cold.

The Arctic is the second-coldest part of Earth. Its average temperature is 32 degrees Fahrenheit (0°C) in summer and –18 degrees Fahrenheit (–28.2°C) in winter.

Ice in the Arctic floats on ocean water, while most of the Antarctic's ice sits on land. Water gets warm faster and more easily than land. This makes the Arctic slightly warmer than the Antarctic.

HOW GLACIERS FORM

Most glaciers are at Earth's poles. But glaciers exist on every continent except Australia. They are in mountainous areas and are called alpine glaciers. Alpine glaciers need a lot of snow in the winter and cool temperatures in the summer. This lets snow and freezing rain **accumulate**.

There are more than 650 glaciers in Alaska. Many of them are in Glacier Bay National Park.

When a layer of snow on a glacier lasts through the summer, it becomes **dense**. The snow turns into small **pellets**. The pellets press closer and closer together. This layer is called firn.

During the next winter, more snow falls. The firn compacts more. Each year, the layers of firn grow and bond together. They become thick, dense ice. As air is pressed out of the ice, ice crystals start to stretch under the pressure. In very old glaciers, these crystals can be several inches long.

Close to 75 percent of Earth's freshwater is trapped inside glaciers. Glaciers cover **approximately** 10 percent of Earth's land area. That equals an area of more than 5.8 million square miles (15 million sq km)!

ICE AGES

An ice age is a long period of time when Earth's temperatures drop. During these times, glaciers grow. Earth's ice ages each lasted for millions of years. In between ice ages, Earth's temperatures rose and glaciers retreated.

57 TO 52 MILLION YEARS AGO
The Earth is warm. Parts of Europe and North America have tropical weather. Trees grow in the Arctic and Antarctic.

52 TO 20 MILLION YEARS AGO
The Earth cools and ice caps grow in East Antarctica. Then a huge ice sheet forms there. In North America, the average yearly air temperature drops by 54 degrees Fahrenheit (12°C).

20 TO 16 MILLION YEARS AGO
Earth experiences a warming period.

16 TO 5 MILLION YEARS AGO
Another ice age happens. Greenland is completely covered by glaciers.

5 TO 3 MILLION YEARS AGO
Earth experiences another warming period. Ocean temperatures get warmer around North America and Antarctica. Trees grow in Iceland.

3 MILLION YEARS AGO TO PRESENT
Earth experiences a cooling period. Northern central areas of Europe become **tundra**. Central China grows cold too.

Cold temperatures keep glaciers solid. But that does not mean they sit still. Forces make glaciers slowly move. The immense power of moving glaciers shapes the land. They carve deep canyons, create lakes, and pick up and deposit rocks and sand as they move.

Heavy glaciers **exert** downward pressure. This pressure causes firn and snow to melt, even without a rise in temperature. So, the bottom of the glacier becomes slick. It begins to slide across the land.

Some glaciers move toward bodies of water. Pieces break off into the water. This is called calving.

20

Valley glaciers flow between mountains.

Gravity also pulls on alpine glaciers. These glaciers slide down mountains toward lower areas. Some can cover 160 feet (50 m) per day. Most move more slowly.

As they move, glaciers grind the land beneath them. They pick up rock, gravel, sand, and mud. The glaciers move them far away from their sources.

Advancing glaciers carve steep valleys and **fjords**. They dig out rounded holes in mountains. They create tall, jagged **ridges**. They also make steep, pointed peaks.

Shrinking glaciers retreat back toward their center. Retreating glaciers deposit bits of rock and soil. Sometimes they leave behind huge boulders. They also leave long hills, called drumlins.

HEATING EARTH

Glaciers retreat during warmer periods. During these times, the summer melt is greater than the snowfall of the winter. Higher temperatures cause more summer melt.

Earth's atmosphere controls its temperatures. It keeps out the coldness of outer space. It traps and holds the sun's warmth. This process is called the greenhouse effect. It keeps the average global temperature at about 58 degrees Fahrenheit (15°C).

Earth's atmosphere allows most of the sun's rays through to reach the planet's surface. As the Earth warms, it **emits** heat energy. But the atmosphere blocks some of the heat from escaping into space. This keeps Earth at temperatures that can support life. Without the greenhouse effect, Earth's average temperature would fall to 0 degrees Fahrenheit (–18°C).

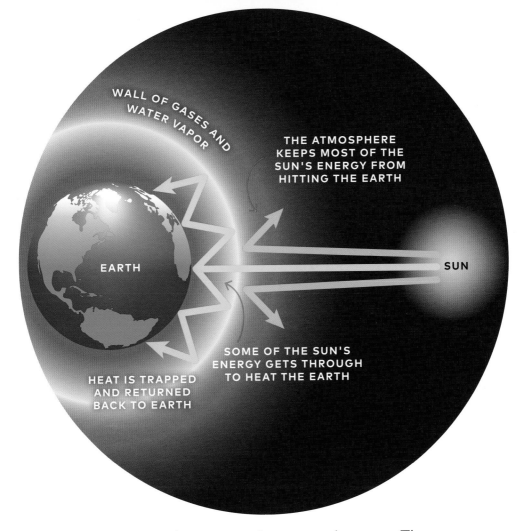

WALL OF GASES AND WATER VAPOR

THE ATMOSPHERE KEEPS MOST OF THE SUN'S ENERGY FROM HITTING THE EARTH

EARTH

SUN

SOME OF THE SUN'S ENERGY GETS THROUGH TO HEAT THE EARTH

HEAT IS TRAPPED AND RETURNED BACK TO EARTH

The atmosphere contains several gases. They include water vapor, **methane**, and carbon dioxide. Carbon dioxide is very important in the atmosphere. It and several other gases control Earth's temperatures. Changes in carbon dioxide levels can greatly affect life on Earth.

MELTING GLACIERS

Looking into a glacier is like looking back in time. Scientists study **cores** of glacier ice. They tell scientists about the world's climate as far back as several hundred thousand years.

Cores contain trapped air bubbles. Scientists **analyze** the bubbles to see how the climate changes from year to year. Ice cores reveal the natural climate changes of the past. They have shown when ice ages happened.

Ice cores can also show scientists the effect of burning **fossil fuels**. Burning these fuels releases carbon dioxide. The carbon dioxide gets trapped in glacier ice.

People began burning fossil fuels in large amounts during the **Industrial Revolution**. This increased the amount of carbon dioxide in the atmosphere. This increase shows in ice cores. Scientists can use ice cores to measure the increase of carbon dioxide over time. In the past 200 years, it has increased by 40 percent.

Car exhaust is a major source of carbon dioxide in the atmosphere.

 With more carbon dioxide, more heat becomes trapped in the atmosphere. This may increase Earth's average temperature by 2.5 to 10.4 degrees Fahrenheit (1.4 to 5.8°C) during this century.

 This puts Earth's glaciers at risk. Since the early 1900s, many glaciers have been retreating farther than they have in the past 5,000 years. Since most of Earth's freshwater is trapped inside glaciers, if they continue to melt, ocean levels will rise. This could cause flooding and other problems around the world.

CHANGING
ICE

CONCLUSION

Temperature controls practically everything on Earth. The sun's energy travels a very long distance to reach us. Its energy transfers to Earth's surfaces. This energy makes atoms speed up and produce heat. It keeps our planet warm. Our oceans remain liquid, while some water is trapped in ice. Life can exist and do well within the blanket of our atmosphere.

Pollution from power plants and other man-made sources can affect the atmosphere and Earth's temperature.

It is also a delicate balance. Small changes in Earth's average temperature can make big differences. Temperatures control Earth's ice ages. During these times, glaciers move and change the land. During

Scientists at the McMurdo Station in Antarctica found ice that is about 8 million years old.

warming periods, glaciers melt. This cycle has been happening again and again for millions of years.

Human activities also affect Earth's temperatures. Massive glaciers have survived hundreds of thousands of years. How will temperature affect them in the future?

FREEZING POINT

EXPERIMENT

QUESTION

Can you pick up an ice cube with a piece of string?

RESEARCH

You already learned about water's freezing point (page 17). What happens when you combine water, ice, and salt? Here's what you'll need to find out:

- glass filled with water
- ice cube
- salt
- 6-inch (15 cm) piece of string

28

PREDICT

Make a guess about what will happen. **Predict** how each material will affect the others. Write it down.

TEST

1. Place the ice cube in the water. It floats to the top.

2. Wet the string. Lay it on top of the ice.

3. Hold one end of the string in each hand. Lift up the string. What happens to the ice cube?

4. Lay the wet string on top of the ice cube again. Sprinkle salt over the ice cube and string.

5. Wait one minute. Lift the string up again. What happens to the ice cube this time?

ASSESS

Was your prediction correct? Why or why not? What would happen if you used a different liquid? What about with a thicker or thinner string? Try it and find out!

GLOSSARY

accumulate – to gather or pile up.

analyze – to determine the meaning of something by breaking down its parts.

approximately – about or reasonably close to.

bounce – to spring up or back after hitting something.

combustion – the act or instance of burning.

core – a part removed from inside an object or mass to learn more about its history or what it is made of.

dense – thick or compact.

emit – to give off or out. An emission is something that has been emitted.

exert – to put forth or bring into use.

fjord – a long, narrow inlet of the sea between cliffs or steep slopes.

fossil fuel – a fuel formed in the earth from the remains of plants or animals. Coal, oil, and natural gas are fossil fuels.

friction – the force that resists motion between bodies in contact.

hydrogen – a chemical element that is a colorless, odorless gas.

Industrial Revolution – a period in England from about 1750 to 1850. It marked the change from an agricultural to an industrial society.

mercury – a silver white, metallic element. It is used in batteries, thermometers, and various scientific instruments.

methane – a colorless, odorless, flammable gas used as a fuel. It forms when organic matter breaks down.

pellet – a small, hard ball.

physicist – a person who studies matter and energy and how they affect each other.

predict – to guess something ahead of time on the basis of observation, experience, or reasoning.

random – lacking a definite plan or pattern.

ridge – a narrow, raised area on the surface of something.

sphere (SFIHR) – an object shaped like a globe.

tundra – cold, dry, treeless land in the Arctic. Below the surface, the ground is permanently frozen.

WEBSITES

To learn more about Science in Action, visit **booklinks.abdopublishing.com.** These links are routinely monitored and updated to provide the most current information available.

INDEX